Copyright

Table of Contents

Hollywood At Its Inception

Hollywood is a place where many individuals aspire to succeed. It is a place where those dreams can come true, and it can undoubtedly be called the land of opportunity. To many people the idea of Hollywood mainly refers to the artists whose job it is to engross us with fantasy and escapism through the magic of films. Some consider mainstream musicians, and other highly sought out artists to be a part of this construct. In any case, many artists and musicians, and actors and actresses, often cross over into each others' worlds, thus making all of them a part of what could be considered "Hollywood".

Hollywood is not just a place in California anymore. It encompasses the film and television industry as a whole. Even at its' founding, Hollywood brought popular cultural topics and people from all walks of life together. Movies often reflect what is going on in the world during a particular time period. In times of war many film directors and writers create pro- or anti-war films depending on the sentiments of mainstream society. Ethical dilemmas and stories of peacetime are also depicted in such films. Individuals who study the history of our culture often feel as if films and television are artistic creations that represent the prevailing sentiments of a given historical timeframe. These so called sociological documents can depict ideologies and play to people's morals and political views. They can also pass on psychological views that portray a social anxiety or a particular social tension, or even cultural views that portray a particular gender, race, etc. Parodies create levity when serious situations affect society.

The first film in the United States was shown in Herald Square, New York City in 1896. The film is celebrated on a commemorative plaque beside the Macy's department store located there. From then on the movie industry began to develop. Up into the early 1900's films were considered to be a novelty. Films lasted no longer than ten minutes and used anonymous actors on set. Those early actors and actresses were not paid millions of dollars like they are today. A typical actor or actress made only about $8 per day and did not receive any credits in the film. The film quality and style of filming made the actors' faces virtually unrecognizable. Therefore no one actor was able to differentiate themselves from the others. All films back then were silent movies.

In 1905 the Nickelodeon entered the market. These were theaters in which patrons paid only a nickel to view a film. The crowd was diverse, in that the poor of society as well as middle class individuals came together to view films on the big screen. By 1914 an actress named Florence Lawrence became the first to become widely recognized and is known as The First Movie Star. She was no longer an anonymous actor holding out for $8 a day. She was a star and earned the likes of $10,000 a week.

Hollywood was becoming a major influence on society. This influence became a concern to religious and civic leaders and the politicians of the day and they set out to stop film production. From this grew the Censorship Board. The Board, headed by William H. Hays, felt the themes presented in film were corrupting the minds of people in general. It sought to protect the people from delinquent activity and illicit lovemaking. They believed that these things came from watching movies. In response to the censorship board many of the Nickelodeons and movie theaters closed down. After the closures, and in an attempt to bring film back into a more acceptable society, Hollywood banned together with moral reformers to create the Voluntary Board of Censorship. The Board was tasked with evaluating films based on sexual and violent content.

As the years have passed Hollywood has become much larger than it's physical size. Some big motion pictures are shot all over the United States and Canada. In the early 1990's the Independent Film industry sprouted up and many Indie films are funded and produced by Hollywood Studios annually. Many big studio films and independent films are made in the United States and Canada. Actors and actresses not filming in Hollywood are still considered Hollywood Celebrities.

Scandals and Mysteries 1900-1940

Though the Voluntary Board of Censorship was formed to help the movie industry, the end of the Great Depression raised questions about the morality of the film industry once again. There were a host of murders, suicides, and other scandals that rocked the face of Hollywood during this era that called into question the morality of films as well. Here are a few scandals that would shape the face of Hollywood society and the movie industry during the time.

Mystery Aboard a Yacht: Thomas Ince

Date: November 15, 1924
Location: Ince's home in Benedict Canyon, Los Angeles, California
Victim: Thomas Ince
Suspect: William Randolph Hearst
Cause of Death: Acute Indigestion

Backstory: Thomas Ince was born Thomas Harper Ince in Newport, Rhode Island on November 16, 1882. Ince began his career on stage at the age of 6. By age 15 he had made his first appearance on Broadway, hitting the stage in the production *Shore Acres*. During his teen years he held a variety of different jobs while working as a part time actor. He also worked as a lifeguard and promoter. Though he was offered some Vaudeville work, it was on an inconsistent basis until he was hired by the Edison Manufacturing Company, a motion picture company. It was during his time at the company that he began to develop a Vaudeville company of his own. It would later fail. In 1906 Ince starred in the Broadway production *For Love's Secret Sake*. It was on the set of this production that he met his future wife Elinor Kershaw.

Soon after the pair married, Ince left his unsuccessful acting career and gained employment with Biograph, another motion picture company, in New York City. A few years later, after a brief stint of underemployment, a friend helped him secure a position at Independent Motion Pictures (IMP) Company. During his employment there he was afforded the opportunity to direct a film. This was the start of his directing career.

After success directing his first film Ince was able to convince the head of IMP, Carl Laemmle, to let him start directing films on a full-time basis. Laemmle was impressed and sent Ince to Cuba. While there he was under the direction of the Motion Pictures Patent Company, he put out a small number of films in many different genres, though Westerns and American Civil War films were his specialty. His successful production career earned him the title Father of the Western.

In 1911 Ince was offered $100 a week to go to California and make Western Films under the New York Motion Picture Co. While working for the company, Ince made some changes to the way films were made. He revolutionized shooting scripts and scene plots to aid in efficient shooting schedules.

In 1912 Ince purchased a plot of land and built what was known as Inceville, his first movie studio. The studio was state-of-the-art. It was equipped with stages, offices, and the like. The studio housed many different sets but mostly sets for westerns. Ince even housed livestock on the property that would later be used in his productions. Actors and actresses came in to shoot films via the Red Trolley Car, while cowboys of the day, as well as native Indians lived on the property. Ince was also the first in Hollywood history to define a producer's role and hold them accountable for the movie's production from start to finish. Before Ince went on to build studios in Culver City he had directed close to 20 films and made over 150 two-reel movies. He went on to produce and direct many more movies.

The Night In Question: On November 15, 1924 Ince boarded the yacht of William Randolph Hearst. Ince was late due to an important business matter. He, along with Charlie Chaplin, Aileen Pringle, Seena Owen, and Dr. Daniel Carson Goodman, among others were aboard the yacht. One guest in particular, Marion Davies, who Charlie Chaplin was said to have been romantically involved with and ultimately became a key player in this incident, was also aboard the yacht. During dinner a special celebration was thrown in honor of Ince's birthday, he was turning 42. During the night Ince began to suffer from chest pains, which the doctor onboard later determined was caused by acute indigestion.

As his condition worsened Ince was taken off the ship by way of water taxi. From there he was taken to a hotel where he was treated by a practicing physician. He told the physician that he had consumed a large amount of alcohol while onboard the yacht. From the hotel Ince was transported home.

November 19th: Three days after Ince was taken off the ship because of his failing health, he was pronounced dead in his home. The cause of death was ruled as acute indigestion.

November 20th: The front headline on the morning edition of the Los Angeles Times read, "Movie Producer Shot on Hearst's Yacht." From then on the stories seemed to spring up from everywhere.

The first accounts implicated Hearst in the incident. Stories swarmed around stating that Hearst had shot Ince in the head by mistake. Many stories have come out saying that Hearst found his mistress Marion Davies having an affair with Charlie Chaplin aboard the yacht. Through many stories one thing remains the same. Many state that Hearst pulled out a gun and fired shots at Chaplin who was lucky enough to get away. The stray bullets were said to have struck Ince who was either in his room, standing on the deck nearby, or trying to step into the middle of the confrontation.

The Investigation: With so many stories flying around, and Hearst in the middle of many of them, the DA's office started an investigation into the death of Thomas Ince. They failed to question several witnesses and took few accounts of the events that night. They only questioned Ince's doctor who was on board the ship and had accompanied him until he reached his home in the nights following. The doctor noted the events that led to Ince's death and the investigation was closed. Though the investigation was closed there is still suspicion surrounding his death.

A Case of Amnesia: Many of the guests aboard Hearst's yacht reported that they had not been there the night of the incident. Charlie Chaplin reported that he only heard about the incident, and went to visit Ince in the hospital later that same week. He also made note that Ince died two weeks after his visit, though Ince actually died two days after he was taken off the yacht. Chaplin attended his funeral services that following Friday. Many of the guests aboard the vessel that night reported seeing Chaplin and other guests, who denied being on the vessel on the night in question. Marion Davies also reported that she too was not there, and that she had only heard about the incident when Ince's wife Nell called her on the night of his death.

Abigail King Loving, Marion Davies' secretary may have also been a suspect in the case. She reported that Ince raped her on the night in question, and was seen with bruises on her body by other party guests. Several years later she died in a mysterious car accident. A suicide note was found in her vehicle that was inconsistent with her handwriting. Even more suspicious was the fact that the accident occurred near Hearst's residence, and she was found by two of his bodyguards.

Immediately after Ince's death his wife ordered his body to be cremated. This allowed for no autopsy to be conducted for further investigation in his death. Soon after she fled to Europe, possibly under the direction, and with money from Hearst.

Conclusion: The case was officially closed, but suspicion still exists.

A Gentle Man: Paul Bern

Date: September 5, 1932
Location: Bern's home on Easton Drive, Beverly Hills, California
Victim: Paul Bern
Suspects: Jean Harlow, Dorothy Millette, IrvingThalberg
Cause of Death: Gunshot wound to the head

Backstory: Paul Bern was born December 3, 1889 as Paul Levy. He was born in Wandsbek, Germany to mother Henriette Levy, and father Julius Levy. Both his parents were of Jewish descent. In 1898 the patriarch of the family decided to uproot his children and wife and move to America. The move was in response to anti-Jewish attitudes in Germany during the time and lack of job opportunities in the area.

At the start of his career Bern was an actor at the American Academy of Dramatic Arts in New York City. This is where he adopted the name Paul Bern. After many years in the city Bern moved in with his common-law wife Dorothy Millette. Due to her emotional and mental problems Bern was forced to leave her in a Connecticut sanitarium. After a few years on stage, Bern decided that he would be best suited in other areas of theater production. In 1920, not long after his mother committed suicide, he moved to Hollywood.

Bern started as a film editor when he first hit the Hollywood scene and worked his way up from there. Many referred to him as the "little father confessor" of Hollywood. He was known to have an open heart, and would console or talk to anyone that needed to confide in him. In 1930 Bern, 42, met 21-year-old actress Jean Harlow. What started as a friendship ended up in marriage in 1932. Soon after Bern began writing and directing films under the direction of United Artists and Paramount Pictures. His work with these "major" studios earned him the opportunity to gain full-time employment as a producer with Metro-Goldwyn-Mayer. Before his death Bern and producer Irving Thalberg produced the box-office hit *Grand Hotel.* The movie went on to win an Academy Award for Best Picture in 1932.

Months Before His Death: In the months before his death Bern suggested to a friend that he had thought about leaving his wife and entering a monastery. It was during this time that he renewed his passport as well, making his travel plans seem likely. He had also been facing financial hardship. He borrowed money from his wife and others in the Hollywood scene.

The Night In Question: September 5, 1932 Bern was found naked and mortally wounded from a gunshot wound to the head. At the scene of the crime police found what they called a "suicide note". The note read:

"Dearest Dear,
Unfortunately this is the only way to make good the
frightful wrong I have done you and to wipe out my
abject humiliation, I love you.
Paul
You understand that last night was only a comedy."
(1)

Many of his fans and other movie goers found out about his death while at the theater. A sign flashing during a holiday show that he had died horrified many of them. In the following days reporters, Hollywood executives, and the police demanded and pleaded with Harlow to provide an explanation. She refused.

Suspects: Jean Harlow - Harlow maintained she knew nothing about why the incident occurred only two months into the couple's marriage. An autopsy report showed that Bern had never consummated the marriage, a fact known to Mrs. Barbara La Marr. Bern had wanted to marry her some years before but she knew that their marriage would only be a mental and spiritual companionship. Harlow found this out three days into the marriage.

Irving Thalberg - Thalberg was Bern's co-producer of *Grand Hotel*, their Academy Award winning film. It was released only three days after Bern's death. A fellow friend, Samuel Marx, some years later stated that on the night of Bern's untimely death that he had seen Thalberg tampering with the evidence at the scene. This was before the police were notified. On September 6th the head of MGM noted that the case would be ruled a suicide, all to avoid a scandal.

Dorothy Millette - Millette was known to have visited Bern the night before his death. Two days after Bern was found, Millette jumped to her death from the Delta King paddle boat. She was his common law wife.

Investigation: A1932 investigation concluded with the police ruling the crime as a suicide.

Conclusion: The case would be re-opened in 1960. This came after screenwriter Ben Hecht called into question the official ruling of Bern's death. He maintained that Bern was having an affair and that the unidentified woman murdered him. He also maintained that MGM covered up the murder by having it ruled a suicide. This was to protect their bottom line and Harlow's appeal at the box-office. The L.A. County District Attorney reopened the case, but soon closed it due to false accusations.

Trials and Tribulations in Hollywood

By the late 1930's there was a change in the industry once again. The Great Depression had hit and movie attendance was down more than ever before. Films of the time tried to reassure people that things would get better and to maintain the national morale, and over 80 million people went to the theater each week. However, film studios were going into debt by the millions. At this time viewing audiences had decreased to almost 40% in some places. In an attempt to stop the financial bleeding, production costs and salaries were cut, theaters also had to resort to lowering admission prices, cash giveaways and other gimmicks to get patrons through the door.

Movies during the Great Depression era were very different from the films produced in the years before. Previous films were social films, or rather films that came straight from the newspaper headlines onto the big screen. Depression films had sad or grim undertones, reflected in the characters represented during the time. They also poked fun at strong political views, sex, and other moral convictions held by mainstream society. This led to what was known as the Breen Bureau in 1934. This bureau was in charge of screening scripts before they went into production and was led by Joseph I. Breen. The code did not allow for nudity, profanity, white slavery, scenes of passion, crime, and adultery, among other things, to be displayed on screen.

During this time the Catholic Church set out on a "united and vigorous campaign for the purification of cinema, which has become a deadly menace to morals."(2) Over 9 million people followed the Church's lead in this boycott. This is when producers and the major studios started to enforce the rules of the Breen Bureau. If a movie could not pass their scrutiny then it would not be played in major theater chains. From the Breen Bureau came many positive things. For one, women were depicted in a wider variety of roles, and directors went in search of new cinematic techniques. Techniques that would avoid censorship, but would still touch on taboo topics.

Scandals and Mysteries 1940-1980

Just as Hollywood was making changes for the better, a new event sent it reeling. World War II had started in 1939. During 1941 a major investigation was launched into the wartime affairs of major Hollywood studios and affiliates. The Senate committee in charge of the investigation was labeled the House Committee on Un-American Activities or HUAC for short. This investigation led to the creation of the Black List. Numerous actors, actresses, and film studio executives were subjected to questions concerning their involvement in communist activities during the war.

Among the 150 people that were subjected to investigation 10 of them, known as the Hollywood Ten, would spend at least a year in prison for their alleged involvement. For this they, and the 150 others under scrutiny, were also blacklisted in Hollywood. They were unable to find employment with any media-based production. The investigation lasted until the 1960's. While there were several investigations into wartime activity and the allegiances going on, a number of scandals also occurred. Here are a few of note.

The Death of a Mobster: Lana Turner and Johnny Stompanato

Date: April 4, 1958
Location: LanaTurner's home in Beverly Hills, California
Victim: Johnny Stompanato
Suspect: Cheryl Crane
Cause of Death: Stabbing

Backstory: John Stompanato Jr. was born October 10th, 1925 to John Stompanato Sr. and his wife Carmela in Woodstock, Illinois. The family had Italian-American roots. Johnny had three siblings, two sisters Grace and Teresa, and brother Carmine. His family had moved from Brooklyn to Woodstock in 1916. Shortly after Johnny was born his mother died from peritonitis. His father would later remarry.

In 1940 Stompanato was sent to Kemper Military School in Missouri. Three years later, after his graduation, he joined the United States Marine Corps. After three years serving under the direction of the 1st Service Battalion he was discharged from the Marines.

A Chance Encounter: In 1956, after a chance encounter, Lana Turner met Johnny Stompanato. At the time Stompanato was a big named mobster who she knew by the name of John Steele. Turner was an up and coming actress many knew as the "sweater girl". At the time of their meeting Stompanato was bodyguard to famous mobster Mickey Cohen and was well known in the "underworld".

Turner was filming *Another Time, Another Place* in Europe, and Johnny made sure to follow her. Rumor has it that while in Europe Johnny began hearing that Lana Turner was having an affair with her co-star Sean Connery. Johnny confronted Connery with a gun on the set of their film. Connery wrestled the gun out of Stompanato's hand and had him deported out of the country. After shooting the movie Turner and Stompanato enjoyed a vacation in a private villa in Acapulco before returning to the United States two months later.

Upon their return to the United States their relationship started to deteriorate. Turner knew that her blossoming career could not be shared with a mobster. When she was nominated for an Academy Award, Turner opted to take her mother and daughter to the ceremony, which made Johnny angry.

The Night In Question: On the night of April 4, 1958 Stompanato stormed into the home of his lover Lana Turner in Beverly Hills, California. An argument began between the two. Johnny made threats to Turner, some of which hinted at killing her. Reports stated that he shouted that he would cut her face to end her career. Turner's 14-year-old daughter, Cheryl Crane, was in the home that night.

Fearing for her mother's safety, and for her own, she went to the kitchen and grabbed a 10-inch kitchen knife. She went back up to the room, and according to her own accounts he ran into the knife.
Some could argue that she attacked Stompanato in an act of bravery, trying to keep him from killing her mother. After he was stabbed he fell to the floor in a pool of blood. Crane called for her mother who in turn called the police. The police pronounced Stompanato dead upon their arrival. They then arrested Crane.

The Aftermath: Lana Turner denied having a relationship with Johnny after the incident, saying that he was a ladies man and he had obviously become obsessed with her. After her denials Mickey Cohen, of the mob, released to the media letters that Turner had sent Johnny. In the letters Turner confessed her love for the man she said was obsessed with her.

Sean Connery went into hiding after the death of Stompanato. The mob believed that he had some responsibility for the murder and Mickey Cohen wanted anybody and everybody involved with the murder to pay with their heads.

Conclusion: Stompanato's death was ruled justifiable homicide and Cheryl Crane became a ward of the state until 1961. Turner went on to star in her last major production titled *Imitation of Life.*

Not So Super: George Reeves

Date: June 16th, 1959
Location: Reeves' home at 1579 Benedict Canyon Drive
Victim: George Reeves
Suspects: Toni Mannix, Lenore Lemmon
Cause of Death: Gunshot wound to the head

Backstory: George Reeves was Mr. Superman himself. Reeves was born in Woolstock, Iowa under the name George Keefer Brewer on January 5, 1914. His parents were Don Brewer and Helen Lescher.The birth occurred five months after they were married and they separated soon after his arrival. Reeves never saw his father after the divorce. Helen married Frank Bessolo, who later adopted Reeves and raised the boy as his own. After a 15-year marriage, Helen's relationship would come to an end once again. After the divorce Helen told Reeves that Bessolo had committed suicide. It was not until his later years in life that Reeves found Bessolo was still alive, though not his biological father.

When Reeves reached high school age he became engrossed in acting and singing. During this time he also took up amateur boxing, but was forced to stop by his mother. It was her belief that if he continued with the sport he may mess up his face, making him ineligible to pursue an acting career.

After high school Reeves went on to study at the Pasadena Playhouse. This is where he was introduced to his future wife. Reeves and Ellanora Needles were married on September 22, 1940. During the marriage the two did not bear any children, and like his mother's past relationships, it ended in divorce.

After his studies, Reeves' career in the film industry began to blossom. He was cast in such films as *Gone With the Wind.* From this film he was offered a contract by Warner Brothers. The studio executives changed his name to George Reeves. While at Warner Brothers, Reeves was cast into several B-films. He starred along with well-known political figure Ronald Reagan, and actor James Cagney. After Reeves was released from his contract he was signed to Twentieth Century Fox.

As the war raged on in the 40's, a number of actors including Reeves joined in on the fight. Reeves entered the Army in 1943 and made a number of appearances in *Winged Victory*, a USAAF Broadway production that gained national attention. After the successful run of *Winged Victory*, Reeves began his work with the First Pictures Unit, a unit associated with the Air Force. While there he made numerous training films.

When the war concluded Reeves made his way back to Hollywood. During this time Hollywood was in despair. Many film studios and production houses were either closed down, or slowly producing and releasing films. Reeves did his best to pick up a few films before fleeing to New York in 1949. While in the city he worked in television and radio.

In 1951 Reeves was offered the television role of. Many people during the time did not have televisions in their home, and believed television would not be successful in the long run. All of these facts made Reeves skeptical of taking the job, but his decision to take the job turned out to be a great one. When ABC purchased the show, it aired to a national audience and Reeves became an instant celebrity.

At the beginning of the show's history Reeves was underpaid, and he was required to adhere to strict guidelines set forth by the network. One of the rules that he and others had to abide by was they were not allowed to accept other roles that interfered with production of the show. This rule prevented them from taking long-term projects. As Superman, Reeves became a role model for the children of the world, and he took his status and power of influence seriously. Reeves avoided cigarettes and kept his private life behind closed doors.

On set Reeves was a real prankster. He also stood up for cast members in times of scandal, and during issues with directors. Low pay continued to be an issue, and the network kept strict guidelines over the cast. This led Reeves to believe he needed to move on with his life and pursue other roles. While ABC tried unsuccessfully to find a replacement, Reeves opened up his own production company. He made one film before ABC called him back to work, enticing him back with the promise of $5,000 a week while the show was in production.

Reeves went back to work as Superman. In 1959 Reeves and his cast mates were to sign a new contract and go into production of a new Superman series. Reeves was promised the right to give input on shows, and be able to direct as well.

While many thought the role of Superman made Reeves happy, friends would later say that Reeves described the role as a waste of his life. It was during his relationship with girlfriend Lenore Lemmon that Reeves reports having financial problems. She started rumors that they planned to be married in Mexico and then travel on a tour to Spain and Australia. Three days later, Reeves was dead.

The Night in Question: June 16, 1959 George Reeves, Lenore Lemmon, William Bliss, Robert Condon, and Carol Ronkel were at Reeves' home located at 1579 Benedict Canyon Drive. Many of the guests had been drinking, including Reeves and Lemmon. At some point in the night Reeves and Lemmon began to argue. As Reeves headed upstairs to his bedroom, Lemmon would later tell officers that she shouted out that he would probably shoot himself.

Sometime between 1:30 and 2a.m. a call was made to the police notifying them of the suicide of Reeves. This was some 45 minutes after a gunshot was heard and his body was discovered by the inhabitants of the home. William Bliss was said to be the first to discover Reeves' body.

When the police arrived on the scene, Lemmon and guests were clearly drunk. The officers went upstairs to find Reeves lying naked in an upstairs bedroom. A pool of blood lay underneath his body, and the gun was positioned between his feet. The wound was a through and through in the head. Blood was splattered on the nearby walls and ceiling. The L.A. coroner ruled it a suicide and closed the case. The police and other officials stated that a failing career and inability to be cast in different roles contributed to the suicide.

Controversy: While the case was closed as fast as it was opened, suspicions by the public and within Hollywood grew surrounding Reeves' death. Evidence suggested someone else could have been responsible for Superman's death. Investigators found shell castings lodged in the floor and other places, which would be odd considering it was a suicide. Also, it took guests 45 minutes to call the police after hearing the gunshot. There was no gunpowder residue found on the actor's skin, which would be present if he in fact shot the bullet that killed him. There was also an absence of fingerprints on the gun.

Suspects: Toni Mannix: She had been Reeves' lover, though Reeves had ended the relationship. Many have speculated she ordered a hit on Reeves because of the breakup. It was later revealed that she made a dying confession in relation to the murder. She claimed she was responsible. A former cast mate of Reeves', Phyllis Coates, later shared that Mannix called her at 4:30 in the morning following Reeves' death. Coates remembers Mannix being in a fit of hysteria over Reeves' death.

Lenore Lemmon: Lemmon may have been a suspect as well. She was rumored to have told a guest after the shooting occurred to tell the others she had been downstairs the whole time. She attempted to be awarded his estate but was denied as they were not yet married.

Conclusion: A formal investigation into the case found no foul play, and the case was ruled a suicide, plain and simple.

Death of a Playboy Regular: Jayne Mansfield

Date: June 29th, 1967
Location: Hwy 90 near Slidell, Louisiana
Victim: Jayne Mansfield
Cause of Death: Traffic Accident

Backstory: Jayne Mansfield was born Vera Jayne Palmer in Bryn Mawr, Pennsylvania April 19, 1933. Her father was a German man named Herbert Palmer, and her mother's name was Vera Jeffery Palmer. Her father died of a massive heart attack when Mansfield was only three years old. Mansfield spent most of her childhood in Phillipsburg, Pennsylvania. After her father's death her mother remarried and moved the family to Dallas, Texas. When she was 13 years old she and her mother took a trip to Los Angeles. Her time there led her to decide that she wanted to be an actress.

While in high school, Mansfield studied a variety of different languages including German, and learned to play the violin and piano. After she graduated she went on to marry her first husband Paul Mansfield. In 1951 their daughter, Jayne Marie Mansfield, was born. Together the two enrolled in Southern Methodist University where they studied acting. The next year the pair moved to Austin, Texas to study drama at the University of Texas. While she held many different jobs on and around campus, Mansfield was fond of the theater and joined what was known as the Curtain Club, an on campus theatrical society. Mansfield also entered a number of beauty contests and won. She was offered her first film role in a B-film called *Prehistoric Women.*

Just a short year later Mansfield and her husband moved back to Dallas. While there they studied acting under Baruch Lumet, until Paul Mansfield was deployed to Korea during the Korean War. Two years later the pair moved again to L.A. to study Theater Arts at UCLA. While at the school Jayne won many beauty pageant titles including Miss California at the local level, Miss Texas Tomato, and Cherry Blossom Queen. The pair would move several more times before the actress caught the eye of a TV producer who helped her land a part-time modeling job at the Blue Book Model Agency.

Mansfield tried her hand at acting starting back in 1954. She was unsuccessful getting many of the roles she auditioned for, until she received her first role in CBS*'s An Angel Went AWOL.* In 1955 Mansfield went on to pose for Playboy Magazine. Her photos were modest, in that she wore pajamas, and only the bottoms of her breasts peeked out from underneath. This spread helped further her career, and helped grow the Playboy name. Mansfield was a featured Playgirl from 1944-1960, gracing the pages of the magazine each February.

At the height of her Playboy success, husband Paul Mansfield sought custody of their child claiming that Mansfield was unfit due to her national exposure in Playboy. The two were divorced in 1958. Just a few months after her divorce from Paul Mansfield she married Mickey Hargitay. That marriage produced her second daughter, Mariska Hargitay, a well known actress, and two sons, Mickey Hargitay Jr., and Zoltan Hargitay. Her last marriage was to Matt Climber, in 1964, with whom she had another son, Tony Climber.

Mansfield starred in a number of films in her early years. She also had a seven-year contract with Warner Brothers in 1955. The contract paid well during that time and landed her several film roles. She would later move to theatrical productions, the most noteworthy being Broadway's *Will Success Spoil Rock Hunter?* After 1959, Mansfield's career began to decline. With a number of pregnancies standing in her way, and inability to land major roles, her six-year contract with Fox was spent loaned out to foreign film studios where she made a number of low budget productions. The last major film in Mansfield's career would be in 1967's *A Guide for the Married Man*, where she enjoyed a cameo appearance and was listed in the opening credits. In all Mansfield appeared in over 30 films.

A Day of Tragedy: On June 28, 1967 Mansfield, her lover Sam Brody, her three children, and her driver, Ronald B. Harrison, set out for New Orleans. They rode in style in a 1966 Buick Electra 225. Mansfield was set to have an early morning television appearance the next day. On June 29 at about 2:25 a.m. Mansfield and family were on U.S. Highway 90 near Slidell, Louisiana. A truck spraying for mosquitos caused a tractor-trailer to slow significantly and blocked her driver's vision. The Buick hit the semi from behind wedging underneath the truck. The driver, Mansfield, and Brody were all killed in the accident. Her three children were injured but all survived. Many reported that Mansfield was decapitated during the incident, but those claims have been proven untrue. Police photographs of the scene show the top of the car torn away, and either a blond wig, or Mansfield's scalp and hair tangled in the windshield of the car.

Conclusion: After the incident the NHTSA began requiring tractor-trailers to have an underride guard, which would later be named the Mansfield Bar.

A Heartthrob Gone Too Soon: Sal Mineo

Date: February 12, 1976
Location: Outside his apartment at 8569 Holloway in West Hollywood, California
Victim: Salvatore Mineo Jr.
Suspect: Lionel Ray Williams
Cause of Death: Stab wound to the heart

Backstory: Salvatore Mineo Jr. was born on January 10, 1939 in Harlem, New York. His father, Salvatore Mineo Sr., was a casket maker and his mother, Josephine Mineo, a homemaker. Salvatore Sr. came to the United States from the Sicilian region of Italy. His mother, although born in the US, was also of Italian descent.

Salvatore Jr., called Sal or Junior, was the third child and also the third son in the family. His older brothers, Victor and Michael were three and two years older respectively. His sister, Sarina, was three years younger.

The family moved to the Bronx when Sal was 9 years old. There he was teased by the local gangs because of his father's business. Sal was able to eventually become a member of a small local gang by smoking a whole pack of cigarettes. From then on he was in. He began down the road so many young boys fall into and began to get into trouble.

Playing the role of Jesus in his school play at the age of 9 introduced Sal to acting. Turns out he was a natural and he loved doing it. While playing baseball with his friends, Sal was noticed by the owner of a dancing school. The owner suggested to Sal's mother that Sal's physical grace and his looks could get him onto television. After some initial reluctance, she agreed to allow him to go to dance school.

Sal worked hard at dance school and soon was making appearances on a local TV show, *The Ted Steele Show*. From there he caught the eye of Broadway producer, Cheryl Crawford. Crawford asked Sal to read one line from a play called *The Rose Tattoo*. She was so impressed with his delivery, she gave him a small part and at the age of 11, Sal Mineo traveled to Chicago to act. *The Rose Tattoo* eventually came back to New York and young Sal came with it. He continued his role until the play closed in 1952.

Later on in 1952, at the age 12, Sal was cast as the understudy of one of the children in the production of *The King and I* starring Yul Brynner. Initially Mineo was intimidated by the actor but then found Brynner to be supportive and helpful to the young actor. When the play closed in 1954, Sal was already a veteran performer. He landed small parts in several television programs and continued to impress.

Sal's older brother Michael also had the acting bug and he asked Sal to accompany him to an audition for a part in a new movie, *Six Bridges To Cross*. However, the casting director noticed Sal and asked him to read for the part of the lead as a young man. Sal got the part and also his first big break. He traveled to Los Angeles to shoot the film and decided to hang around LA once shooting was done. He had heard about another new movie starting called *The Private War of Major Benson*. Again, he auditioned and was awarded the role of a cadet colonel.

Mineo was gaining more and more interest from the entertainment industry and more and more popularity with the young movie going audiences. In 1955 at 16 years of age, Mineo tried out for a part in a new movie called *Rebel Without A Cause*. The movie centered around the difficulties experienced by teenagers and their relationships with their parents and each other. Two other young actors had been cast, 16 year old Natalie Wood and 24 year old James Dean. The movie became a huge hit and Sal was nominated for an Academy Award for Best Supporting Actor. The death of his friend Dean in September of 1955 hit Mineo hard.

Mineo went on to act in another huge hit, *Giant*, in 1956 and several more films and television programs. During this time, in an effort to capitalize on his popularity, he began recording records. He had the perfect voice for teenage love songs and many of his recordings became hits. His albums sold over a million copies.

In 1960, at the age of 21, Mineo was cast in a film by Otto Preminger called *Exodus*. Mineo played a young Jew who had escaped the Nazi concentration camps in World War II and moved to Israel after the war. The cast included Paul Newman, Eva Marie Saint and a young starlet named Jill Haworth. Jill's character was the love interest for Mineo's in the film and the two began a relationship off screen too. The film was another huge hit and Sal won a Golden Globe for his work and was again nominated for an Academy Award as Best Supporting Actor.

By late 1960's, however, Mineo's career had cooled considerably. He was able to get a few guest roles on television shows such as The Patty Duke Show, Combat, and S.W.A.T. He found himself having financial difficulties and was forced to sell almost everything he owned, including a home he had bought for his parents back in New York.

He never gave up, though, and in 1976, at the age of 37, he went back to the theater. He was cast in the play *P.S. Your Cat Is Dead* in San Francisco and received excellent reviews. The play was successful in San Francisco and when it closed there, it was moved to the Westwood Playhouse in Los Angeles. Mineo retained his part and moved back to LA, leasing a small apartment in West Hollywood.

Mineo's relationship with Jill Haworth was short lived but they remained lifelong friends. Sal never married and during the 1960's he began to acknowledge his attraction to other men. Being homosexual in the 1960's was career ending so he was very careful to be circumspect in his relationships. There were rumors that he and James Dean had a relationship but Mineo later noted that he had not realized his bisexual nature until years after Dean's death.

The Night in Question: At approximately 9:30 p.m. on February 12, 1976, Sal Mineo was returning home after a rehearsal of the play *P.S. Your Cat Is Dead.* He had parked his blue Chevy Chevelle in his garage and was walking outside to the door of his apartment when he was attacked and stabbed once in the chest. 9-year-old Monica Merrem, who lived in the apartment building along with other neighbors heard cries for help. She reported seeing a man with long dark curly hair running away. Other neighbors reported seeing an Italian or Mexican man with dark curly hair and still others reported seeing a white man with long dark blond hair.

Mineo was lying curled up on the ground with a long trail of blood coming from his left side. A neighbor attempted mouth-to-mouth resuscitation but the stab wound went to his heart and he died almost immediately.

The coroner's report indicated Mineo died from one stab wound to the heart. It also noted several puncture wounds on Mineo's buttocks, purportedly from hormone shots to revive his flagging sexual performance. Other puncture wounds, however, suggested drug use.

Police Investigation: Police initially thought the crime was a drug purchase gone bad, also possibly a homosexual hate crime. They quickly dropped the drug deal gone bad scenario and concentrated on the homosexual theory. They investigated other homosexuals and bisexuals in the film industry. That trail however led nowhere. The case went cold and was dropped. Mineo's fans criticized the police for not continuing to work on the case.

Sixteen months after Mineo's death, a woman named Theresa Williams contacted the police. She told them her husband, Lionel Ray Williams, had come home the night of the killing with blood on his shirt. He told her he had just killed Sal Mineo with a hunting knife. He said the motive was robbery but when Mineo's cries for help alerted the neighbors, he ran before getting any loot. Mrs. Williams gave her statement to the police then went home and killed herself.

Lionel Ray Williams was a pizza delivery man in 1976. He had a long history of crimes including robbery and check fraud. At the time his wife talked to the police, he was in prison in Michigan for check fraud. In January 1978 he was extradited to California to stand trial.

The Trial: The trial of Lionel Ray Williams began on January 9, 1979 in the Beverly Hills Municipal Courthouse. Williams was charged with 1 count of 1st degree murder, 1 count of attempted robbery and 10 counts of robbery, other crimes the police were able to pin on him.

The prosecution called Allwyn Price Williams, Lionel Williams' cellmate in Michigan. Of no relation to each other, Price Williams testified that while they were incarcerated Lionel had bragged about killing Mineo. The Prosecution also called L.A. County Medical Examiner Dr. Thomas Noguchi. His testimony consisted of using a duplicate knife (provided by Williams' wife before she died) to show that it fit exactly into the wound.

The defense attorney was able to get Price Williams to later admit that he lied to get out of jail. He also admonished the jury to not assume the duplicate knife is exactly the same, since the actual weapon was never found. He also reminded them that Williams' wife is not available to corroborate nor deny her earlier statements, since she is dead. He then called the three neighbor witnesses who all gave differing descriptions of the man they saw running away. Finally, he stated that since Williams is a black man, he does not fit the descriptions of long brown or dark blond curly hair. In response, the Prosecution produced an old picture of Williams with long straightened and died light brown hair.

Conclusion: On March 16, 1979, Lionel Ray Williams was found guilty of murder plus 10 of the 11 robbery charges. He was sentenced to 51 years to life in prison. He served 11 years of his sentence and was paroled in 1990. He was not free for long however, and has been in and out of jail since. His current whereabouts are unknown.

Some believe Williams took the fall for someone else. They believe the real killer is still out there and that they got away with murder.

No one knows what successes Sal Mineo would have enjoyed had he not been mercilessly killed in cold blood.

Risky Behavior: Bob Crane

Date: June 29, 1978
Location: Winfield Place Apartments Scottsdale, Arizona
Victim: Bob Crane
Suspect: John Henry Carpenter
Cause of Death: Bludgeoned to death

Backstory: Bob Crane was born Robert Edward Crane on July 13, 1928 in his hometown of Waterbury, Connecticut to Alfred and Rosemary Crane. Crane found his love of music early in life, playing the drums in junior high. He often led drum parades with many of his friends, even becoming a member of the marching band upon entering high school. At some point in his high school career Crane was afforded the opportunity to play for the Connecticut Symphony, and Norwalk Symphony Orchestra's youth programs.

Crane graduated from Stamford High School in 1946 and two years later he enlisted in the National Guard. While in the National Guard, he married Anne Terzian. Together they had three children. He served two years in the National Guard before being honorably discharged in 1950.

After his release from the National Guard, Crane went straight into broadcasting for WLEA in New York. In order to limit the effect he had on the ratings of their flagship WCBS, CBS took him off the airways in New York City. He went on to broadcast on two other stations in Connecticut.

They later moved him to KNX in Los Angeles, where they hoped he would increase the station's ratings. While working the morning show at KNX, Crane gave it all that he had. This earned the show the top spot and it became the number-one morning show in the L.A. area. With guests like Marilyn Monroe and Frank Sinatra hitting the airwaves, Crane was dubbed "The King of the Los Angeles Airwaves." (3)

As a result of his broadcasting career Crane developed a taste for acting. His acting ambitions led him to guest star on the *Twilight Zone* series and *Who Do You Trust?* among other great shows of the time. One of Crane's most memorable roles was on the sitcom *Hogan's Heroes.* The show was a comedy series centered around a German P.O.W. camp. The series was popular during its stint on the airwaves, and lasted six seasons from 1965 to 1971. For his role, Crane was awarded two Emmys. Crane had divorced his first wife, Anne, in 1970. It was on the set of the show where Crane met and married his second wife Patricia Olson.

After *Hogan's Heroes* ended Crane went on to star in two Disney films, and starred in and directed a play titled *Beginner's Luck*, which toured dinner theatres around the country for five years.

Risky Behavior: It was known that Crane liked sex, and most importantly liked to videotape his sexual activities. Crane had met John Henry Carpenter, a regional sales manager for Sony Electronics, and the two became friends. Crane often introduced Carpenter as his manager and the two would frequent bars and pick up women. They would later lure them to private locations and videotape their sexual encounters. Some woman knew they were being filmed, while others would only find out later.

The Days Before: June 26th, 1978 Crane and Carpenter were in good spirits. The two were seen swimming at a local pool area, before going to Crane's home and watching some of his sexy home videos. At 4:00 p.m. Victoria Berry, an actress in the play *Beginner's Luck*, invited Crane and Carpenter to a barbeque. At 6:00 p.m. the pair showed up to the barbeque together.

June 27th, 1978 12:30 p.m. Carpenter left the DynaTronics electronic equipment store to visit Crane at home. At 3:30 p.m. the two had their photos taken together at a photography studio, before going back to Crane's apartment. While at the apartment the two exchanged jokes, and looked at half naked pictures of women. Later that night, accompanied by two women, Crane and Carpenter went out to dinner. At 11:00 p.m. that night Crane and Carpenter ditched their dates and headed over to Bobby McGee's for drinks.

June 28th, 1978 Crane and Carpenter's relationship had begun to deteriorate. On the 28th, they had lunch in Scottsdale. A waitress at the restaurant noted that there seemed to be tension in the air between the two of them. Even some of Crane's fellow cast mates remember the actor being distracted that same night during his performance in *Beginner's Luck.*

The Night in Question: June 29, 1978 At around 2 p.m. Victoria Berry, came to Crane's apartment for an appointment. While she maintains that their relationship was more of a sibling relationship she confessed to the police she had slept with Crane on more than one occasion. Upon her arrival at his home she knocked on the door. After getting no response she tried the doorknob and found the door unlocked. When she opened the door she discovered Crane's naked body.

Blood covered the entire wall before her, and he was curled in the fetal position with a cord wrapped around his neck to form a bow. Investigators later found that Crane had been bludgeoned in his sleep before the cord was tied around his neck. The weapon was never found nor identified. A coroner's inquest would note that the force had to come from a very strong individual, presumably male.

Prime Suspect: Though a long list of possible people could have motive for Crane's murder, Carpenter was suspect number one. After their lunch on the day before the murder, Carpenter quickly returned to L.A. On the day Crane's body was discovered Carpenter made a number of calls to Crane's home. At one point a detective answered the phone and Carpenter did not seem surprised by the fact that the police were there.

The police launched an investigation and examined Carpenter's rental car. In the car the police found evidence of dried type-B blood, which was the same type as Crane's. However, there was not enough evidence to charge Carpenter, and as DNA testing was not yet available in 1978, the case remained unsolved.

In 1989 the police ran a DNA test on the blood sample found in Carpenter's car. The test report however came back inconclusive. In 1992 after Crane's case had been reopened, investigators uncovered photos of Carpenter's rental car. They noted what appeared to be a piece of brain matter on the door panel of the car. Though the physical evidence had been lost, the judge ruled the photograph, along with expert witness testimony, to be admissible in court, and Carpenter was indicted on murder charges related to Crane's death.

The Trial: At Carpenter's trial Crane's son revealed that Crane, before his death, had confided in him. Crane told him that he wanted to cut ties with Carpenter and continued to tell him that for several weeks, noting that Carpenter was becoming obnoxious and he could no longer deal with him. His son also went on to say that Crane called Carpenter the day before his murder to end their friendship.

The defense argued that the case could not be proven beyond a reasonable doubt. After all there was no physical brain matter on hand to investigate, and only pictures with no way to determine what the speck actually was. In the end the jury decided the case in Carpenter's favor and he was deemed not guilty, due to lack of evidence.

Conclusion: Carpenter died in 1998 continuing to maintain his innocence. The case remains unsolved to this day.

The New Hollywood

After the 60's, Hollywood rid itself of the censorship code under the Breen Bureau and moved to the Motion Picture Association of America Film Rating System that is used today. Some of the minor studios identified a shift in the viewing population from adults to a younger audience, aged 16-25. When the major studios discovered the impact that appealing to a younger crowd had on the industry, they decided to change their strategies and also focus on a younger audience. Therefore, many films during this time period reflected the values and prevailing ideologies of a younger audience and shifted away from traditional values.

Genres used in earlier times were also revisited during this period. Crime films, westerns, and the like were often retold with a critical viewpoint, or enhanced to reflect modern day views. Television also became a mainstay in American culture, bringing Hollywood to the small screen and into many peoples' homes.

During the 70's a shift to fantasy films began. Such films were based on the future, law and order and the human spirit. Films like *Superman, Star Wars* and other such films utilized special effects, action, and story lines that depicted good versus evil to appeal to the masses. Even sports centered films made a rise in the industry, though many thought they would be a major failure at the box office. Films also addressed important social issues such as racial equality ,the changing roles of women, and the transformation of the family dynamic.

Another major shift in film production was the birth of the Indie film industry. Today films are produced all over the world and actors and actresses are considered 'Hollywood celebrities' regardless of their filming location. World markets are becoming more and more important to the film industry. Other countries are gaining more access to American films and this has caused a shift in the decisions being made. Whether a film will appeal to foreign markets is now one of the considerations used to determine if a film will even be made. Also, due to language limitations, the plots of movies made today are being kept to some of the most basic concepts recognized all over the world. Themes such as good versus evil and right versus wrong are common.

Scandals and Mysteries 1980 - Present

With the expansion of movies being produced worldwide, the people involved in filmmaking are coming from all walks of life and cultures. Many entertainment professionals come to the United States to become rich and famous. They bring with them the attitudes and beliefs of their home countries. But people are people no matter where they come from and many of the mistakes and foibles people make are universal.

The scandals that have rocked Hollywood over the years can and do happen to any person no matter their background. Here are some of these scandals.

Innocence Betrayed: Dorothy Stratten

Date: August 14, 1980
Location: 10881 West Clarkson Road, West Los Angeles, California
Victim: Dorothy Ruth Stratten
Suspect: Paul Leslie Snider
Cause of Death: Shotgun blast

Backstory: On February 28, 1960 in the Salvation Army Hospital in Vancouver, British Columbia, a baby girl was born to Simon and Nelly Hoogstraten. They named her Dorothy Ruth. The Hoogstratens were immigrants from Holland. A son, John Arthur followed in 1961. The Hoogstratens separated when Dorothy was three. Nelly Hoogstraten was left to raise her children herself. Money was tight. They lived in a rough neighborhood but Dorothy stayed out of trouble. Another daughter came along in 1968. Louise Beatrice was born on May 8, 1968, five years after the Hoogstraten's separated. Louise's father is said to have been one of Nelly Hoogstraten's employers with whom she had an affair.

As a teenager, Dorothy attended Centennial High School in Coquitlam, a small municipality outside Vancouver. To help her mother pay the bills, she worked part time at the local Dairy Queen.

Paul Leslie Snider was a minor car show promoter and hustler in the Vancouver area. His activities were not always above the law and the Vancouver police viewed him as a part-time pimp.

One day in 1977 he and a friend walked into the Dairy Queen where Dorothy happened to be working. He took one look at Dorothy and is said to have remarked that he could make a lot of money with her. He was 26. She was 17. He immediately overwhelmed her with attention, the pretense of wealth and with promises of more to come. He groomed her for a modeling career.

In 1978 Playboy Magazine began its hunt for their Playmate of the Year. Dorothy was underage and not legally able to pose nude without a parent's consent. Snider forged her mother's signature and had the nude photos taken anyway. The photos were sent to Playboy in California and they immediately sent for her. She did not win Playmate of the Year, being new to the industry, but she was named Miss August 1978 and was paid $10,000. Dorothy worked as a Playboy Bunny while she studied acting and auditioned for parts. She was becoming more and more popular within the industry. Her star was rising. About this time she shortened her name to Stratten.

Snider, however, was considered a hanger-on and was excluded from many of the parties and photo shoots where Dorothy was included. Feeling he deserved the credit for discovering her and fearing he was losing his meal ticket, he become insanely jealous.

Dorothy began to have concerns about Snider but still felt some loyalty to him for his previous efforts. They became engaged. While she took acting lessons and worked as a Playboy Bunny, he fumbled around trying to get her jobs and despite his clumsy attempts to fit into Hollywood society, he was always an outcast while her naturally outgoing and friendly personality continued to attract attention.

One day in 1978 at a party at the Playboy Mansion she met Peter Bogdanovich, a successful and wealthy film director. He was immediately smitten. Sensing her cooling feelings for him, Snider insisted they marry. So on June 1, 1979, when Dorothy was 19, they were married in Las Vegas. Snider forced Stratten to sign a contract entitling him to half of all her money and property for the rest of his life, whether they were married or not.

In 1980 Dorothy Stratten became Playmate Of The Year. Stratten and Snider moved to a larger home in West Log Angeles that they shared with a friend, Dr. Stephen Cushner. Meanwhile, Snider spent money and lived lavishly beyond their means. He continued to devise his own promotions. All were miserable flops. He started carrying a loaded gun. Privately he was scorned by those he was trying to impress. Stratten, on the other hand, was asked by Bogdanovich to read for his new movie, *They All Laughed.* Needless to say, she got the part.

Stratten and Bogdanovich quickly fell in love and she and Snider separated. She went to live in Bogdanovich's mansion and began to enjoy the good life away from Snider's constant harassment and phone calls. Snider had Stratten followed by a Private Investigator named Marc Goldstein to get proof of her affair with Bogdanovich. Dorothy had hopes of reaching a fair settlement with Snider because she felt some loyalty to him for all he had done for her.

On Wednesday, August 13, 1980, Snider bought a 12-gauge Mossberg pump shotgun from the classifieds and told his friends it was for home protection.

The Day in Question: August 14, 1980 Stratten and Snider agreed to meet that day at their previous home for what she thought was going to be a discussion of a financial settlement for their divorce. Marc Goldstein, the Private Investigator who was following her watched her enter the home at 12:30 p.m. He called Snider to see how things were going. Snider answered the first call saying everything was all right but subsequent calls went unanswered

Snider's newest protégé, a young woman named Pattie Laurman, and her friend came to Snider's home during the afternoon but since Snider's door was closed, they left again without knocking or calling out. Marc Goldstein sat outside the home until 11:00 p.m. He finally called Dr. Cushner asking him to check on Snider and Stratten.

Shortly after midnight Cushner opened the door and found the bodies of Dorothy Stratten and Paul Snider. Stratten was nude, kneeling face down on the corner of the bed. She had a massive wound on her face above her left eye and her left pinky finger was missing. She had tape marks on her wrists. There were bloody handprints on her buttocks and thigh. She was in full rigor.

Snider was also nude lying face down on the floor. A shotgun was lying under him. There were blond hairs gripped in his hand. He too was in full rigor with a wound between his eyes. Both bodies had black ants crawling on them.

Snider had built a bondage sex chair that he planned to sell to the porn industry and Los Angeles sex shops. The one prototype he had built was in the room with tape still on it.

Police Report: The police speculate that Snider and Stratten fought physically due to the hair in Snider's fists. Snider then brutally raped Stratten. He then placed the shotgun to her head and shot her point blank. Her left hand was probably brought up to her face to try and protect herself and the pinkie finger was shot off by the blast. Snider then strapped her dead body to the machine and raped her from behind. He finally moved her to the bed then killed himself. Snider's hands were too bloody for the investigators to retrieve any gun powder from them so there is no concrete evidence that he pulled the trigger.

The coroner's report for Snider lists the cause of death as "questionable suicide/possible homicide". (4)

Stratten's purse was on the on floor in the upstairs living room with a note inside in Snider's handwriting stating that he needed money. Stratten was carrying $1,100 and Snider had $400 at the house.

Aftermath: Stratten was cremated and buried at Westwood Memorial Park in Los Angeles, California. Her family chose a quote from Ernest Hemmingway's A Farewell To Arms as her epitaph. Snider is buried at Schara Tzedeck Cemetery in New Westminster, British Columbia, Canada. As a final insult, Snider's family successfully sued for Stratten's estate since the two were still married and Snider was her beneficiary.

Two movies about Stratten, *Death of a Centerfold: The Dorothy Stratten Story* starring Jamie Lee Curtis as Stratten, and *Star 80* starring Mariel Hemingway were released in the following years. Neither were big hits.

The studios refused to release Bogdanovich's movie, *They All Laughed*. He decided to release it himself. It was a flop and nearly bankrupted him.

In 1988 Bogdanovich married Stratten's younger sister, Louise. They divorced in 2001 after 13 years of marriage.

Something Out of West Side Story: Natalie Wood

Date: November 29th, 1981
Location: Catalina Island, California
Victim: Natalie Wood
Suspects: Robert Wagner, Christopher Walken
Cause of Death: Accidental drowning and hypothermia

Backstory: Natalie Wood was born Natalia Nikolaevna Zacharenko on July 20th, 1938. Her parents were Russian immigrants who moved to San Francisco in search of better opportunities. The actress grew up speaking Russian and English. Her mother aspired to be an actress, but with the responsibility of raising her children and wanting to remain true to the Russian Orthodox Church, she pushed her aspirations on to Natalia.

At a film shoot in Santa Rosa, California, Natalia was noticed in the crowd. Soon after, her mother moved the family to L.A. so that her daughter could pursue a career in acting. Natalia became a child star at the ripe old age of five years old. Her first role would last 15 seconds in the film *Happy Land* in 1943. Irving Pichel, a Hollywood director, noticed her and two years later, he called Natalia's mother asking that Natalia attend a screen test in L.A. The studio executives changed her name to Natalie Wood. At seven she landed a role alongside Orson Welles as a German orphan in the film *Tomorrow Is Forever*. She was then chosen for another major role in *Miracle on 34th Street*. This role would launch a successful career for the child star.

Natalie Wood transitioned nicely into a teen star. Her first major role would be as Ann Morrison in *The Pride of the Family*, and then in *Rebel Without a Cause*. She would go on to be nominated for an Academy Award for her role. Wood grew into a versatile adult actor. In 1957 she married Robert Wagner. She starred in major films and was nominated for another Academy Award, as well a Golden Globe, in the Best Actress category. After a string of successes, in 1961 Wood's career began to decline. Being cast into a leading role in *Splendor in the Grass*, and then *West Side Story* in 1961 revived her career. It was around this time that Wood and Wagner divorced. She would later go on to marry British producer Richard Gregson in 1969. The marriage would last three years before ending in divorce. Wood re-married Wagner some three months later.

The Night in Question: November 29, 1981 Wood, along with husband Wagner, actor Christopher Walken, and others were aboard Wood's boat *Splendour* for a weekend trip to Santa Catalina Island, California. During the night Wood fell overboard and drowned. It would not be until 8 am that morning when authorities discovered her body floating a mile away from the boat.

The Autopsy: The autopsy initially revealed that Wood had bruising on her body and arms. An abrasion was also found on her left cheek upon further examination. Her blood alcohol content was 0.14% at the time of her death. Two medications, that increase the effects of alcohol in the body when taken in combination, were also found in her system. Her cause of death was ruled accidental drowning and hypothermia.

Suspect Number One: Robert Wagner reports that he and Wood had an argument right before her death. This accounts for the bruises found on her body at the time of the autopsy. The captain of the boat also revealed that an argument had ensued between the two on the night of her death, a fact that he kept quiet until 2011. The captain hinted at the fact that Wagner may have been responsible for the incident.

An Alternative Theory: Christopher Walken was aboard the boat that night. Until 1997 the actor was determined to keep his silence about the death of Natalie Wood. In a Playboy interview the actor discussed his theory. He maintained that Wood was alone the night she died. He explained that a dinghy was hitting the side of the boat that night and Wood probably went out to move it. He notes that there was a ski ramp right before you get to the dinghy and the area was slippery. Several people, including himself, had slipped in the area earlier. He noted that Wood could not swim and that she probably slipped and hit her head before falling overboard.

Rumors: Rumors continue to swirl around the events of that night. Wagner has stated that it was he and Walken who were having the loud argument and that Wood may have left to get away from the argument. Others speculate that Walken and Wood were having an affair and Wagner found out. Also, cries for help by a woman were allegedly heard in the area that night.

Conclusion: In 2012, audio recordings were discovered and added to the evidence list. The recordings were of Lana Wood, Natalie Wood's sister, describing a drunken call she had received from the boat's captain, Dennis Davern. He claimed that Wagner had pushed Natalie, unintentionally sending her overboard. Wagner then refused the let the captain search for her while she cried for help.

The coroner would also write an addendum to Woods death certificate stating that the cause of death was drowning and other undetermined factors.

Madam to the Stars: Heidi Fleiss

Date: June 1993
Location: Los Angeles, California
Incident : Police raid on her home, and Imprisonment

Backstory: Heidi Fleiss was born December 30, 1965 in Los Angeles, California. Her parents were Paul and Elissa Fleiss. Between the two they had four children, and two adopted children. Her parents were very cultured and loved the outdoors. The summer months were filled with trips to historical sites and camping.

Heidi began working at a young age. At 12 she was a young girl babysitting kids in her neighborhood. Many recalled her being a friendly and responsible young woman. She was so good at her job, that requests for her services became hard to manage. In order to keep up with the high demand Fleiss employed her friends to work for her under her babysitting service. It was from this experience she knew she would be successful at business.

The same success could not be seen in her academics. She received poor grades in both junior high school and high school. She began paying students to help her with her work and cut class often. She dropped out in 10th grade.

After dropping out of school Heidi was employed at a number of jobs, until she meet millionaire Bernie Cornfeld in Beverly Hills, California. She wanted his lifestyle and earned herself a position as his personal secretary. The two eventually became romantically involved, though the relationship would end in heartbreak. Cornfeld taught Heidi many things but could not remain faithful through their relationship. After the relationship fizzled Heidi moved back to Los Angeles where she practiced real estate for several years before deciding it did not generate enough money to keep her in the lifestyle she had become accustomed to.

Before her 22nd birthday she was introduced to the world of prostitution. Her then boyfriend, Ivan Nagy, introduced her to Madam Elizabeth Adams. The woman ran a prostitution ring that earned itself the reputation as the most prosperous prostitution service in the Los Angeles area. The Madam played host to the stars and was looking for someone to take over the business. Adams took Heidi under her wings and taught her every facet of the business. Heidi even spent a short time serving as a prostitute. She quickly rose through the ranks and became an assistant Madam, tasked with hiring a more attractive set of ladies to aid the business.

Although Heidi helped turn major profits, she only saw a small percent of the proceeds. After much success Heidi, along with her friend Victoria Sellers, moved into a home located in Benedict Canyon. Heidi grew Adams' client list. Among the clients were some of Hollywood's major directors, actors, royal figures, and heads of state.

At some point Adams and Heidi's relationship began to break down. She ultimately ended up going into business for herself. She employed only the most attractive women who sought her out. Some of her girls were college students, and even a former Miss U.S.A. contestant. She made seven million dollars in her first year of operation and her girls retained 40% of the profits they earned. Her service also extended to international markets, as she loaned her girls out abroad to service the wealthy.

The Night in Question: On June 9th, 1993 the police raided Heidi's home. They listed a multitude of charges against her including pandering. In August of 1993 she appeared at her arraignment where she pleaded not guilty to the charges she faced.

The Trial: A trial ensued that same year. At the trial, members of the jury were evenly divided, with some believing the police had entrapped Heidi, and others feeling that she was justly apprehended. Heidi faced 3 years in prison when the jury decided she was guilty on three of five charges against her. She appealed the decision, and received a reduced sentence of 18 months. In 1994 Federal charges were brought against her and her father. The charges ranged from tax evasion to money laundering. She was sentenced to 37 months in prison. All together she served 20 months in prison.

The Scandal: After Fleiss' arrest, many big names in Hollywood and around the world were suddenly faced with the possibility that she would open her 'Black Book'. It supposedly contained the names of the clients her business had catered to over the years. Some of the biggest and most famous names in Hollywood were said to be in her book. One name was accidently released because of Traveler's Checks found in her purse. That person was Charlie Sheen. Although pressured to release the names, Fleiss refused and continues to keep them secret to this day.

In Conclusion: Heidi Fleiss insists that she is making a move to Nevada. While there she wants to open a Stud Farm, in which she wants to employ the sexiest men alive to please women.

East Coast, West Coast: Tupac Shakur

Date: September 13, 1996
Location: Intersection of Flamingo Rd. and Koval Lane in Las Vegas, Nevada.
Victim: Tupac Shakur
Suspects: Orlando Anderson, of the Southside Crips gang, and Bad Boy Records
Cause of death: Internal Bleeding from gunshot wounds

Backstory: Tupac Shakur was born Lesane Parish Crooks on June 16, 1971 in East Harlem, New York. Both his mother Afeni Shakur, and father Billy Garland, were members of the Black Panthers in the 60's. Shakur was surrounded by a family full of criminals to say the least. Just a month before his birth his mother was acquitted of over 150 conspiracy charges against the United States government, his grandfather was a convicted murderer, and his stepfather was a fugitive from the law featured on the FBI's most wanted list for several years.

In 1986 Shakur was uprooted from Harlem and taken to Baltimore, Maryland. He studied two years at Paul Laurence Dunbar High before continuing his studies at Baltimore School for the Arts. While there he performed in a number of plays, and studied jazz, acting, and ballet. He also discovered his love of rap, winning many competitions for his rap skills. In 1988 the Shakur family moved once more to Marin City, California. This is where his rap journey began, earning him a contract with Atron Gregory and working in the group Digital Underground. A few years later he went solo.

Many of his records took a stance on political issues, and issues facing the young black male in society. Shakur knew what life for a black man was, and figured there was nothing better to talk about than what he had lived through. This was the source of much controversy in his life, though he never strayed from his beliefs. In addition to his music, he also appeared in 10 movies.

Making Enemies: In 1995 Shakur recorded under Death Row Records with his new group Outlaw Immortalz. Shakur recorded several albums under Death Row, many of which earned great success. In June of 1996 the East Coast West Coast rivalry began. It started when Shakur's group released a track titled *Hit 'Em Up*. The record was aimed at rapper Biggie Smalls. On the track Shakur alludes to the fact that he slept with Biggie's wife, and talked about rival record label Bad Boy Records. The track was based on a 1994 attack on Shakur at Quad Studios, which an associate of Bad Boy Records was said to have orchestrated. Shakur and Suge Knight, the CEO of Death Row Records, became closer. The rivalry was not only fueled by the attack on Shakur in '94, but also an incident in '95 that ended with Knight's close friend, Jake Robles, being murdered at the Platinum Nightclub in Atlanta. Sean Combs, CEO of Bad Boy Records, was assumed to be behind it as well.

A Grim Premonition: Two years before Shakur's death, he sat down with Entertainment Weekly for an interview. Writer Benjamin Svetkey asked Shakur where he saw himself 15 years from now. Shakur responded by saying, "sprinkled in ashes smoked up by my homies." (5) He went on to say that he was, "like a tragic hero in a Shakespeare play."(6) He noted that on every level people used him, and as such he had no friends, and likewise no resting place.

The Night in Question: September 7th, 1996 Shakur attended the Tyson fight at MGM Grand in Las Vegas. While leaving the match an alleged gang member of the Crips gang was spotted on the premises by Suge Knight. Shakur, due to another incident earlier that year, attacked the gang member known as Orlando Anderson.

After the incident, which had been caught on tape, Knight and Shakur entered Knight's black BMW 750iL sedan, heading towards Club 662. At approximately 11:00 p.m. Shakur and entourage were stopped on Las Vegas Blvd by police and later fined and let go. Ten minutes later their vehicle stopped at the intersection at Flamingo Road. While waiting at the light a white Cadillac pulled up beside their vehicle, a window was rolled down and a spray of gunfire erupted in Shakur's direction. Shakur was shot several times, with one bullet piercing his right lung, and another hitting him in the pelvic region. Knight was grazed by a bullet to his head.

The pair was rushed to University Medical Center of Southern Nevada. Shakur was hooked up to life support, and doctors put him in a chemically induced coma. The rapper died six days later from his injuries. The official cause of death was listed as internal bleeding. His body was cremated the next day, and like his premonition foretold, he was, "mixed with marijuana and smoked by members of the Outlawz." (7)

Six months later, on March 9, 1997, The Notorious B.I.G., an East Coast rapper also known as Biggie Smalls, was killed in a drive by shooting. It is believed the shooting was in response to the murder of Tupac Shakur.

A Likely Culprit: Six years later in 2002 an investigative reporter led a yearlong investigation into the case. The investigation noted that it was likely that members of the South Side Crips of Compton had designed the attack on Shakur. This was in response to the earlier fight at the MGM Grand. Anderson, whom he had gotten in a physical altercation with, was considered responsible for Shakur's fatal wounds, though he would later be dismissed as a suspect and be killed in a gang shooting years later.

Stunning Revelations: In 2011, Los Angeles Police Department detective Greg Kading wrote a book titled *Murder Rap*. In the book he makes note of some stunning revelations from his investigation into the Shakur/Smalls murders while still with the LAPD. In his book he notes that a Southside Crips boss, Duane Davis, reportedly admitted that he was riding in the white Cadillac that was used in connection with Shakur's murder. Davis told the detective that Combs offered to pay him a million dollars to take out Shakur and Knight. Davis's nephew was Orlando Anderson, whom Davis identified as the shooter of the fatal bullet.

Other facts have come out in relation to the case as well. Shakur's former fiancé Kidada came out stating she asked Shakur to wear his bulletproof vest on the night in question. She stated that he refused to wear it because it was too hot.

A member of the Outlawz, Yak iKadafi, was riding in the car behind Shakur's and was said to be able to identify the shooter. He had planned to step forward to the police and tell what he knew but two months after Tupac's death he was murdered in a New Jersey housing project.

Conclusion

Hollywood has come a long way since its early days. The film industry is constantly going through changes as it tries to create new and more entertaining films for its audiences. So many movies are made outside of Hollywood, including both blockbusters and Indie films, that Hollywood is no longer just a place but it is a symbol for the whole industry.

The one thing that has not and will never change is the human element. People, whether rich or poor, famous or infamous, will continue to live their lives, make good and bad decisions and be the fallible, unpredictable and ever fascinating creatures they have always been. The drive to be famous, to be 'known', will continue to provide us with people whose stories, scandals and murders we can read about, wonder about and be tantalized by.

As time goes by, the facts of these cases can change. New information becomes available, people forget (or remember), some decide to come clean, deathbed confessions occur and the conclusions at times are left open to interpretation.

References

1.   http://www.examiner.com/article/jean-harlow-and-paul-bern-a-scandal-hollywood-s-golden-age

2.   http://fan.tcm.com/_Hayzed-Hollywood-II/blog/6520736/66470.html?createPassive=true

3. http://en.wikipedia.org/wiki/Bob_Crane

4. http://longform.org/stories/death-of-a-playmate

5.   http://www.huffingtonpost.com/2013/12/04/tupac-animated-interview_n_4379823.html

6.   http://www.huffingtonpost.com/2013/12/04/tupac-animated-interview_n_4379823.html

7. http://en.wikipedia.org/wiki/Tupac_Shakur

Dear Readers,

I want to thank you for purchasing my book. I hope you enjoyed reading about the scandals and murders in this book as much as I did researching them. If you enjoyed this book please share it with family and friends.

Thank you for your support.
Sincerely,

Mike Riley

Be sure to check out Mike's other books:

Hollywood Murders and Scandals: Tinsel Town After Dark

"In the late afternoon, her friends recalled, Monroe began to act strangely seeming to be heavily under the influence. She made statements to friend Peter Lawford that he should tell the President goodbye and tell himself goodbye."

Murders Unsolved: Cases That Have Baffled The Authorities For Years

"The body was wrapped in a plaid blanket, and placed inside a box that had once held a baby's bassinet purchased from J.C. Penney's. The boy was clean and dry, and recently groomed. However, he looked to be undernourished. Clumps of hair found on the body suggested he had been groomed after death."

Made in the USA
Columbia, SC
02 August 2021